Traditional Tales
of Mull

by
Peter Macnab

Illustrations by Pat James

Brown & Whittaker

1998

Published by Brown & Whittaker Publishing
Tobermory, PA75 6PR

in partnership with the Trustees of the Isle of Mull Museum

ISBN 0 9528428 7 4

Set in Times New Roman 10 pt and printed in Tobermory, Scotland

Contents

REFERENCES

The author himself; information gathered during a lifetime from friends and
relatives on Mull.

Information supplied by the late Seton Gordon, that great authority on the
folklore of the Highlands and Islands.

The Island of Mull, its history, etc: John MacCormick, (Alex. Maclaren
& Sons, Glasgow, 1923).

PUBLISHERS' INTRODUCTORY NOTE

The old stories and legends of Mull have fascinated Peter Macnab throughout his long
life. Recently there has been a revived interest in the old stories and folklore of the
Gaelic west. It is very much hoped that the publication of the present selection will
encourage Muileachs young and old to remember and re-tell many of the stories that
are not here. If the Mull Museum could hear and record more of the old Mull tales,
perhaps one day it might be possible to put together another collection of the old
stories that tell us so much about the way people used to live - the funny stories that
made them laugh and the ancient tales that they believed.

The Publishers.

MULL: ITS FOLKLORE AND SUPERSTITIONS

'Morvern for sword play, Mull for a song' as the Gaelic has it: and I would add '....for a story', for surely among all the isles of the Hebrides none has such a variety of history, folklore and superstition; and yes, sadness and oppression. The Celtic imagery of folklore and superstition is inherited from the days of the so-called Druids down through the ages and the great days of the Clans. No written records were kept, but were handed down by word of mouth through those men of prodigious memories, the seannachies, the 'Wise Men" of the clans.

However, memory is not infallible. And over hundreds of years it was inevitable that the records of incidents became distorted or exaggerated, until now some simple event long ago exists as a story involving ghosts, fairies, giants and monsters ... the whole fantasy of folklore and superstition. I'll give you an example. I have investigated the cairns marking the great leaps of the Ghillie Reoch (described later). Probing into the soft bogland at each cairn I can confirm that stones deeply sunk well below each cairn mark not only the occurrence of some event here long ago, but that it has been maintained for hundreds of years. Marking what? Perhaps where a clansman was cornered and simply managed to fight his way out. Nothing more. No reference to the history of Mull would be complete without telling the story of the rise of the Clan MacLean of Duart and its offshoot, the MacLaines of Lochbuie. In Gaelic it says - 'the MacDonalds were the warriors, but the MacLeans were the gentlemanlv fellows.' Gentlemanly, yes, for they fought well and fairly, with neither the wild ferocity of the MacDonalds nor the craft of the Campbells, always fighting for whoever they held to be the true king of Scotland in the direct line. This was one of the reasons for the frequent opposition to governments by the Scottish clans, for instance against Cromwell's domination, and in the Jacobite cause.

Yes, the MacLeans were bonnie fighters. Perhaps their greatest achievement was at the battle of Inverkeithing in 1651, when under their leader, Hector, along with their ally the Buchanans they held off the crack troops of Cromwell's army for four hours, until their chief was killed and only 50 survived out of 800 MacLeans.

Dispossessed of their lands in 1691, which were taken over by the Campbells, Duart Castle and the surrounding fields were restored as the *'Duthchas'* or heart of the clan once again, when bought back in 1912 and rebuilt by Sir Fitzroy D. MacLean, 26th chief.

Camacuals.

5

THE ORIGIN OF THE CLAN GILLEAN

There is an old story about the origin of the clan. There were three brothers in Ireland who were left destitute when their inheritance was seized by a greedy uncle. Moving on to Scotland, one brother settled in North Ayrshire, where he died. The other two, Eachann and Lachlan (Hector and Lachlan) drifted up to the MacDougall lands of Lorne, where they were invited to stay at Dunollie Castle, that looks over Oban Bay, for the traditional period of a year and a day. They passed the time in hunting and the pastimes of the day, becoming close friends of the MacDougalls.

A servant at the castle was hostile to them and tried to smirch their character by complaining to MacDougall that they were feeding their hunting dogs with stolen food beside the Dog Stone that stands below the castle at the edge of Oban Bay. The base of this pinnacle of rock is said to have been undercut by the friction of the chain of Ossian's great dog Bran which was tethered there long ago. The MacDougalls refused to believe the servant's story. Anyway, when the year was up, MacDougall suggested that the brothers should go over to Mull and seek favour with MacDonald, Lord of the Isles and owner of the Mull lands. Having rid themselves summarily of the lying servant, who had rowed them over to Mull, they wandered up to the then populous but remote Glencannel, at the head of Loch Ba, met up with MacGillivray, head of a small unit and a protégé, of the Lord of the Isles, but his hospitality was so grudged, and he even insulted them over the food, that they stabbed him to death. This, they were aware, would bring retribution from the MacDonalds, the chief being absent at the time; so learning that he was returning to Mull they launched a boat, drew up beside the galley, and quickly leaping on board they threatened MacDonald with death if he refused to forgive them for their action. Not only did the MacDonald give his word, although forced under duress, but he offered the two brothers the usual hospitality for an extended visit. Soon two weddings took place between the two brothers and the two MacDonald daughters; from those unions descended the two houses of Duart and Lochbuie. How Mull came into the hands of the MacLeans was through the cunning of a nurse. Eoghann's first-born boy, along with his nurse, was in the company with MacDonald. In a fit of generosity he hinted to the nurse that he would be glad to bestow some gift on his grandson. The nurse replied that a generous gift would be 'Erisgeir and its islands'. On the spur of the moment this was agreed to by the chief who was to regret it when the nurse pointed out that the islands around Erisgeir (which is nothing but a rocky islet between Gribun and Staffa) were in fact Mull, Coll, Tiree, and the rest. Having given his word the chief could not retract. That, as the story goes, is how the MacLeans became established in Mull. A likely story but more accurately, the true facts of the MacLean connection starts in the 13th century with the warrior Gillean of the Battle Axe. The Duart connection dates from 1390, when MacDonald, Lord of the Isles, gave the warrior's descendant

Lachlan MacLean custody of Duart Castle, and became founder of the House of Duart. The name of the ancient warrior is perpetuated - in the manner of other clan names in the very name MacLean, MacGillean, senior descendant of Gillean, becoming the shortened 'MacLean'.

Eachann married a daughter of the Lord of the Isles, and it might corroborate the Erisgeir story that a large portion of the MacDonald lands was granted to the first-born son of the union. The first chief of the Lochbuie MacLeans - changed to MacLaine - was Eachann Reoganach, son of John Dubh, fourth chief of Duart. There is an amusing old description of the names of the early chiefs "As dogs lapping soup, the names of the MacLeans; "Eoghann-Lachlann-Eoghnann Lachlann."

TRAGEDY ROCK

Here is one of the saddest stories in Mull. On the strip of flat land at the foot of the 1,000ft cliffs of Gribun, there stands Clach na Leannan, the Stone of the Courting Couple, just 50 yards inland from the road where it passes the first farm you will come to from Salen direction, with a windblown elder tree at the gable. This stretch of road on the south side of Loch na Keal (correctly Ceall, cells of the missionaries) can be rather terrifying, in one quarter-mile stretch cut along the base of the overhanging cliffs with a drop into the sea below. Rock avalanches occur after frost or heavy rain, boulders frequently come down when started off by sheep movements higher up. On one occasion a boulder weighing, I'm sure, all of a ton bounced down not 50 yards ahead of my car. Vehicles have been isolated here until road gangs were able to clear the blockage in front and behind. That gives you some idea about the dangers of these crumbling cliffs. The late Seton Gordon told me the true story which he had learned from the local farmer, Archie MacFadyen. It was about the year 1700, in the autumn, that John, a young man who came from the Ross of Mull, was engaged as a shepherd at Gribun. He was betrothed to Rona, daughter of the local blacksmith. The wedding took place on the day after his arrival. The young couple had been fortunate in obtaining a tiny but cosy cot-house that stood opposite the farmhouse where the wedding was celebrated. It was built in front of a great outcrop of rock that safely deflected stones falling from the cliff above.

The wedding celebrations went on until dawn in the barn of the farmhouse. Now, the weather had been threatening on the day of the wedding, with a storm building up. It broke through the night with a great wind roaring in from the sea accompanied by torrents of rain. As time went on, the newly-weds slipped out unnoticed and hurried over to their little home. With the noise of the storm, piping and celebrations, no-one heard the dreadful sound in the night when the great

outcrop split, and a huge section rolled down the few intervening yards, coming to
rest on and completely flattening the cot-house with the young couple inside. There
they lie to this day with just a few flowers springing up against the rock in their
memory.   Archie MacFadyen told Seton Gordon that his grandmother used to
describe how, during her lifetime, the ends of some of the rafters were still to be
seen projecting from under the boulder. That would be mid or early nineteenth
century.

MACKINNON'S CAVE

West of Gribun the cliffs draw back into a wide amphitheatre enclosing a fine stretch of arable land ending at a low sea cliff. Here, a short distance beyond Balmeanach farm, the great entrance to Mackinnon's Cave can be reached after a safe scramble down to the boulder beach. At high tide the sea penetrates for a few yards into the floor of the cave, which stretches for an unknown distance inland, blocked at the end by rockfalls from the roof. A tiny waterfall drops just beside the entrance. The cave is named after the abbot MacKinnon whose tomb lies within Iona Abbey. Seeking complete peace for his meditations, he moved from the island of Staffa, where there was too much noise from the sea, echoing in the caves, and came to this dark, silent retreat. After 50 yards the passage opens out into a chamber where lies a huge flat table-like mass of stone, known as Fingal's Table. The passage continues until blocked by the rock-fall. Dr Johnson and Boswell were deeply impressed by the magnificent proportions of the cave when they visited it.

The tradition connected with this cave is shared by other caves in the Hebrides, but this is how it earned an evil reputation. Many years ago a party of local men decided to trace the windings of the cave, one group walking above, guided by the sound of bagpipes played by the group below exploring the cave, lightly armed and with blazing torches. All went well for a time until suddenly the piping faltered, and the piper seemed to have turned back. It was an ominous message he attempted to send up when he started to play the tune that says - "Would that I had three hands, two for the pipes and one for the sword", but it became discordant and finally ended. Apprehensive, the men above armed themselves heavily and entered the cave, well lit up with many torches. The first indication of trouble they found was the piper, hacked to death. As the party proceeded with caution, they came across the bodies of their friends similarly dispatched. Sadly, the searchers returned to the entrance. It was apparent that the cave was the abode of malevolent beings, who had been temporarily kept at bay by the holy abbot. As far as the explorers were concerned, the creatures ware charmed by the pipe music and, having killed the rest of the party, they allowed the piper to retire as long as he was able to play. When he tired and his fingers faltered, he, too, met his fate. It is said that a dog that accompanied the explorers emerged from under the hill at Tavool miles away on the other side of Ardmeanach, with every hair on its body singed off!

The tale of the dog could be no more than corroborative detail intended to add artistic verisimilitude to the narrative. But could it have been that if such an exploration did take place, the deaths were the result of bad air trapped far in the recesses? Still, who knows. Beware the evil spirits when you visit the cave.

THE NUNS' CAVE

Talking about caves, a more acceptable story comes from the Nuns' Cave at Carsaig, in the south of Mull. It, too, lies under high sea cliffs of fascinating geological interest, about a mile along the rough shore west of Carsaig Bay. Wild goats may be seen on those cliffs (as well as on the cliffs of Ardmeanach or Laggan), escaped or loosened when the people were turned out of their homes at the time of the Clearances. Beyond the Nuns' Cave lie the fantastic Carsaig Arches, where columnar basalts have been worn into arches and shallow caves.

The Nuns' Cave is a wide shallow cave above high-water mark, with many symbols on the west wall, apparently carved by the monkish masons of Iona who carved slabs of grey sandstone 'won' from the horizontal bed on the shore in front of the cave. This they converted into grave slabs and some of the ornamental designs in Iona Abbey.

The cave was so named after it is said to have given shelter to the nuns ejected from Iona after they had been cast adrift by the fanatical Reformers.

LADY ROCK

It is said that there was only ever one bad Duart chief. Perhaps this was Lachlan Cattanach. Outside the south-east corner of Pennygown chapel, near Salen, you will see two recumbent carved slabs. These, I was told, cover the graves of this chief and his wife. They were reputed to have dabbled in witchcraft, even burning live cats whose squalling conjured up the Evil One who was obliged to do their bidding. For that reason they were refused interment in the holy ground within the chapel itself where there are still many small slabs to be seen. While witches were not allowed interment in holy ground, the holy Church, in its compassion, allowed them to be buried at crossroads, whose design of the cross was the next best thing. Of course as a precaution, those plebeian witches had to be pinned down with a stake through the heart to ensure their evil influence would trouble the community no more. However, all that is an aside. Lachlan Cattanach was married to a daughter of Campbell of Argyll; but as time went on and she failed to give him a son and heir, he decided to plan her decease. Unwilling to invoke trouble through some obvious act around the estate, he arranged quietly to have her conveyed to Lady Rock, a tidal reef just south of Lismore lighthouse, halfway over from Oban. Here she was left at the mercy of the incoming tide and Duart could bewail her loss through a drowning accident. Unfortunately for him, she was seen by a passing fishing boat, rescued, and landed over on the mainland of Argyll, where several places are claimed to have been the exact spot where she was set ashore. From there she made her way to her home at Inveraray. Meantime, although lacking a body, MacLean held a mock funeral where he showed every sign of sorrow. Correct me if I'm wrong; but I think "Eleonara" is the title of the poem by Thomas Campbell in which he describes in romantic terms the act and the sequel. The treacherous Lachlan was later assassinated in Edinburgh by Sir John Campbell, brother of the unfortunate lady, who had waited with patience until a suitable occasion presented itself to avenge the attempted murder of his sister. Could this have been that chief with the bad reputation?

THOMAS CAMPBELL

Thomas Campbell, later to become Poet Laureate, spent several of his early years as tutor to a family at Sunipol, Calgary. Mull left a deep impression on him which is revealed in some of his later poems such as "The Pleasures of Hope." His romantic poem "Lord Ullin's Daughter" describes the tragic fate of Ulva chief MacQuarrie eloping with the daughter of disapproving MacLean of Knock, who in pursuit saw the boat in which they were escaping to Ulva lost in a sudden squall. This could not have been the short ferry we know today, but the long exposed crossing of Loch na Keal from the Gribun shore to Torloisk. I was told that at the edge of the shore below Oskamull, before the growth of summer covers everything, you can trace a rough ring of stones where the lady was buried. I never found this.

THE HEADLAND OF THE OLD WOMAN

Caliach Point is the extreme north-westerly corner of Mull. When out in the lobster boat with Alick Ban, he once told me the story behind the name: further, he took the boat close in to the grim rocks where in a small open space he pointed out the isolated massive rock shaped like an old woman. The story he told me went as follows:

An old woman was once collecting shellfish here when she could gain access at low tide. She was so successful that she forgot about the incoming tide and found herself cut off under the cliff. However she risked the dangerous climb and did manage to struggle to the top of the cliff. Returning home, she boasted about how clever she had been to do this with no one to help her. As a punishment for her selfish boast, instead of having given thanks for her preservation, she was turned into a rock, and there she sits to this day.

THE GHOSTS OF SUNIPOL

I have already referred to Sunipol House and its connection with Thomas Campbell, the poet. It is a substantially built house standing near the edge of the cliff north of Calgary, looking across the open sea to the distant islands of the Hebrides. It was used as the manager's house in the days of my grandfather.

At one time strange goings-on were said to have taken place around the house. Repeatedly, stones up to fist size appeared, apparently as a result of no human agency, and the place gained the reputation of being haunted. My grandfather, when he lived there, used to speak of this phenomenon, but in explanation rather than in apprehension.

A story became current locally when the occupant was a man Campbell - no connection with the present Campbells round about - that when he ran short of money he used to disappear for months, returning well in funds again. In explanation, he simply explained that he had (as he put it in the Gaelic) 'taken a leap out to Australia'. However, the rumour spread that in Australia he had indulged in some underhand practices, waylaying miners returning from the gold diggings and doing some bushranging, but more to the point, he had joined posses of bounty seekers and was paid for each aborigine he dispatched. As a result of this persecution, the ghosts of those unfortunate natives had followed him to Mull and reminded him of his actions by bombarding the house with stones.

The explanation was less grim. When the unchecked Atlantic gales blew in, the wind was so forcefully funnelled into the clefts and chimneys of the cliffs that quite large stones were picked up and blown over the top of the cliff, to fall around Sunipol House. On Caliach Point, just a mile or two to the west, the mountainous waves regularly wash far over the top of the 100ft cliff, on the top of which little grass can grow. In fact, along the whole western cliffs of Mull, streams descending are halted and blown right back over the top of the cliffs like smoke, until from a distance they seem to be on fire.

THE TOBERMORY GALLEON

About 400 yards out from the New (MacBrayne's) Pier at Tobermory, under 60ft of water and deeply embedded in the silt lies the Spanish galleon blown up in 1588, or what is left after the subsequent attentions of nearly forty expeditions vainly seeking the great treasure said to have been on board, including the pay chests of the Spanish army that failed to invade England. Independent Scotland was of course a neutral country. This great ship was in fact the *San Juan de Sicilia*, a large merchant ship hired as an armed unit of the great Armada. fleet. But what I wish to describe are the circumstances in which she was blown up by an internal explosion when she was on the point of setting sail and resuming her voyage to Spain after a lengthy refit.

The first theory is that an undercover agent from the English government contrived to have her blown up; secondly, that an emissary of MacLean of Duart, who had been sent on board to demand a final settlement of the costs of re-fitting, was seized and confined near the magazine. Desperate to discipline the greedy Spanish by any means in his power, he managed to lay a train of gunpowder into the magazine and blew himself up along with the ship.

But of the tales handed down from the Mull of those days, I prefer the story that she was blown up by an army of ferocious cats. Wait and I'll tell you what happened. On board there was a ravishing Spanish princess. Actually, such a lady is said to be interred over the Sound of Mull in Morvern. Now, when MacLean of Duart boarded to discuss terms for refitting, he saw the princess and they both fell violently in love. Why, sometimes they were not seen for days.

Along at Duart Castle, Lady MacLean was furious when she heard about it, and set about an effort to destroy ship and princess, always sparing the life of her husband to meet her wrath, She contacted several practitioners such as the Tiree witch and the Doiteag Muileach, but they had no luck, blaming their failure on the number of holy crosses on board. In despair, Lady MacLean consulted the Shuil Gorm, the famous blue-eyed witch of Lochaber. She submitted the job was no bother to her, so she cast the necessary spells and called up a great army of huge, ferocious cats. They swum out to and boarded the ship, and clawed every single person to death, sparing only Duart to escape in a small boat. When he was confronted by his lady, doubtless he was sorry he had not gone up with the ship!

One terrified seaman rushed down to seek safety from the feline attackers, with one big brute on his heels as he reached the magazine deck. Here sparks from the cat's fur set off loose gunpowder and up went the ship!

A final and tamer theory is that a quantity of damp powder had been spread about to dry on the deck. Through some carelessness it became ignited and spread to the magazine.

THE SKULL

There is a possible sequel to the destruction of the Armada ship. The explosion must have been violent, for the body of a cook is reported to have been hurled on to the steep slope not far from MacBrayne's Pier beside a spot still known as the Cook's Cave; just a hollow in the slope. In modern times, a new owner came to the Western Isles Hotel that stands above the pier. Rummaging at the back of a dusty cupboard he discovered a very old human skull which was considered negroid. Thinking it would be a useful object for discussion in the bar he proceeded to nail it up. At the first stroke of the hammer he experienced the most sudden and inexplicable headache, which continued as long as he was trying to pass the nail through the skull. Undoubtedly, he thought, the skull must carry some ancient curse, perhaps from the galleon. Anyway, he secured it in a weighted container, took it out in a boat and sunk it in the deep water of the Sound of Mull, which seemed a satisfactory conclusion.

BLOODY BAY

Just round from Tobermory Bay, beyond the lighthouse, Bloody Bay is ringed round with high cliffs falling straight into the sea. Here in 1480 took place the greatest clan naval fight in the history of the Hebrides, when John, a weak Lord of the Isles, assisted by the MacLeans of Duart, was soundly beaten by Angus Og, who was thoroughly contemptuous of his father John's weakness and hoped to restore the prestige of the Lords of the Isles. The sea is said to have run so red with blood that the bay was given the name. I read somewhere that human bones were found in a cave under the cliffs accessible only from the sea. Perhaps survivors had managed to swim there for safety and been unable to escape.

LOCAL MONSTERS

South of Tobermory, on Aros estate, there lies the shallow Loch na Meal, the loch of the monster. Knowing of its presence, local people, apprehensive of its emergence, treated the loch with loads of quicklime, with no obvious success. Even when it was drained in part about 150 years ago it remained undiscovered. Perhaps it overheard the plan and moved in time to Loch Pealach, the eastern of the three Mishnish Lochs.
Fortunately, it has ever since lived a life of obscurity.

A NEW YEAR PRESENT

Long ago there was an inter-clan custom to exchange a communal gift with a neighbouring clan at the New Year. Usually a few good cattle beasts. This time the MacLeans had sent a fine little herd to the MacKinnons of Mishnish who held that part of Mull until squeezed out by the MacLeans in later years. In return the MacKinnons sent such a small and miserable selection that so insulted the MacLeans that they promptly drove them back to their donors. Arising from this controversy, a minor affray took place between the two clans over to the west of Glengorm (Sorne in those days) and I have been told that several victims of the fight are buried under small mounds at the junction of the old Dervaig/Glengorn road where it meets the track from below the Carnan an Amais, the top Mishnish Loch.

THE WATER-HORSE

Malevolence was not always the work of supernatural beings. All this talk about water reminds me of the well-known story of the waterhorse (or -bull). Why, you even get a similar tradition in China.

A young maiden is walking beside a loch or pool in a river. Before her she suddenly sees a handsome young man - but beware! If she enters into conversation with him, in a flash he turns into water horse, forces her on to his back, and rushes into the water, where she disappears for ever. Always look first for traces of water weeds about such a presentable person, and if you see as much as leaf, take to your heels and be safe. Or it might simply be the water horse itself in the guise of a quiet pony grazing by the water side, an obvious invitation for a gallop: but once mounted in the saddle, the victim cannot dismount and is carried into the water, vanishing for ever.

THE PIPER'S WELL

One of the most remote corners of Mull is Treshnish, west of Calgary, where lies the little old hamlet of Haunn near the coast. Two hundred years ago it was a populous place with good arable land and grazings for herds of cattle, all gone now with the people who were cleared from the land. The story I heard must have come down from the days when bows and arrows were used in ancient wars. Anyway, there was always a cattle minder to watch the movements of the cattle and guard against marauders. Conditions appearing quiet, one day the cattle minder decided to take a few hours off and try to pick up a few fish off the rocks below Haunn. When he returned to duty, to his mortification he saw raiders just disappearing with a selection of the best animals. Feeling guilty, he decided to follow them up and redeem his neglect by dealing with the raiders and recovering the cattle. Being an expert archer, he slipped home and collected his bow, but in his haste he could only lay hands on three arrows. He hurried after the raiders, who could only go at the speed of the herd. He was able to distinguish just three men, so he said to himself he would have to be very careful with the use of his three arrows. Evening was drawing on, but he was able to ambush them, and letting fly an arrow at the nearest man he saw him drop with the arrow through his heart.

In the darkness the remaining two were safe enough, and they camped overnight among the cattle, that would give warning of the approach of a stranger. The archer wormed his way silently to the top of a little bluff within long bowshot of the group and began a long vigil. When daylight came the two raiders gathered the herd and prepared to move. The cattle minder, only too well aware that he had only two arrows left, waited his chance until one of the men paused for a space, so with the greatest care he took aim and again his arrow went truly. One raider left, but he was well-armed, and a confrontation in the open was impossible as the man started to prod the herd towards what we know as Ensay today, where his friends would be waiting. This man was widely known as an expert piper. Becoming over-confident he halted for a drink at a well - a natural spring, dropping his guard just long enough for the watcher to come into bowshot. The final arrow went home and the raider was dead. Ever since that spring was known as Tobar-na-Piobaire, the well of the piper.

The cattle-minder rounded up the little herd and successfully drove it back to Haunn. From a distance the main party of raiders had seen their comrade drop, but fearing that the cattle minder was just one of a larger pursuing party, they gave up and made off. When he returned proudly with the fine cattle he had redeemed his neglect; in fact he was hailed as something of a hero when the people heard what he had done.

THE STILL CAVE

On your way from Calgary to the fair lands of Torloisk, before you descend the Tostarie Brae you will see to the right a tall, gaunt ruinous building. This is Reudle schoolhouse, where on the wall of the one big schoolroom you will still see the graffiti of a past age, such as sailing ships. Children used to come in from miles around, even up to the early years of the 20th century.

Before the bracken smothers everything you can trace the lines of 'lazy-beds' where the schoolmaster once raised a few crops. Passing the building and bearing left you will see a wide valley opening out that extends to the edge of the cliffs. You pass two ruined hamlets, Glacgugairidh and Crackaig and admire the craft of the people who first put up the clever stonework. Bear left to the edge of the cliff at Crackaig and you can follow the line of an old track winding down the steep slope, going along the raised beach and descending to the rocky shore by a gully in the 80ft cliff. A few yards to the right you will see the entrance to what I call the Still Cave. The cave goes in, dry underfoot, for about 40yds. At the entrance are the foundations of a large illicit still, a platform about 17ft wide with a 7ft hemispherical hollow in the centre in which blazed the furnace that heated the 'Black Pot.' A flue opened underneath that kept the furnace alive. It was operative until well into the 19th century, and I believe certain of my old relatives were not unconnected with it, took a pride in it and kept the metalwork well polished.The whole operation was highly ingenious. In front of the entrance a turf wall had been built which hid any glare from the furnace from the few passing ships. The smoke rose against the dark cliff and dissipated. A tiny burn was diverted to fall over the front and designed to cool the pipe leading from the black pot, condensing the distillate and dripping it into the collecting vessel. All the equipment could easily be made by the local blacksmith, and of course the secret was kept within the villagers above.

The quality must have been very good, in fact, I believe the product may have had two distillings for refinement; so good that the operators even rowed and sailed over to Ireland, where it competed well in the land of the poteen. Detection by the gaugers was almost impossible through the remoteness, the perfect concealment and the secrecy around it. The last time I visited it I found a few fragments of the old kegs at the far end of the cave.

A BRUSH WITH THE KING'S MEN

I was told the following story about an encounter with the 'King's Men' as they were called, the Revenue officers, whose duty it was to end illicit distilling. One day the operators were sailing in their skiff over to the thirsty islands of Coll and Tiree with a full load of kegs. Halfway over, past the point of no return, they spied the revenue cutter some way behind pursuing them under full sail and slowly overtaking. However, it was still some way off when the skiff rounded the point and in front of them lay the sandy bay with all the people anxiously waiting, watching and prepared. The skiff was waved in. Men gathered round it and carried it bodily up the beach and placed it among their own boats lying above high water mark. Women were waiting with pails of water which they splashed freely over the boat and its neighbours, so it was well disguised. Boys had been waiting near the beach with a herd of cattle which they drove across the sand, effectively obliterating the marks left by the boat party. Everyone scampered away, and as the cutter came foaming round the point, all that could be seen was a line of boats well drawn up, people hoeing the potatoes up on the machair and two old men sitting mending lobster pots. The revenue officer dashed ashore with several of the crew and demanded if the two men had seen a skiff passing. They pretended not to understand English, causing further delay. When questioned by a Gaelic speaker in the crew, they replied truthfully, yes, they had seen no skiff passing the point. Seeing everything apparently innocent and normal, the officer turned and shouted - "Quick! Back to the boat. The rascals are making for the Outer Isles!" With all sails set, the cutter departed on its vain pursuit.

That night the Mull men were heroes and a happy time was had by all!

MCLUCAS'S CAIRN

This cairn stands at the summit of the Tostarie Brae overlooking some of the finest views in Mull, just a mile or two beyond Reudle schoolhouse, It became known as McLucas's cairn after a man of that name had found near it a poor man who had died at the roadside, and carried the body on his back down to the houses at Torloisk.

MACARTHUR'S HOUSE

At the foot of the tortuous steep descent, opposite the first farmhouse you come to, you will see the ruins of a substantial house and a few outbuildings, and half a mile beyond it to the west the prominent wall of that well-preserved fort - Dun Aisgean. This was once the property of MacArthur.

A Torloisk man, he was entrusted by the laird of Torloisk to travel to Edinburgh and bring back the vital title deeds and records of Torloisk. In those days, the person who possessed the actual documents had the complete rights of ownership, so the mission was of the greatest importance to the Torloisk inheritance.

However, all this was known to some party with the ownership of the estate in mind, and the faithful MacArthur discovered he was being followed. Without sparing himself he hurried on the return journey, but as fast as he pressed on, so did his pursuers. He was fortunate in finding without delay a ferry over to Mull from the mainland, but not to be denied, so did the others, who caught up so fast that when he reached the River Ba, hunter and hunted were on opposite banks. Again MacArthur escaped and managed to reach the safety of Torloisk, when his pursuers gave up and slunk away.

As a reward for this faithful man, the laird presented him with this house and a fair piece of ground in perpetuity.

THE PIRATE OF TORLOISK

The daughter of the laird of Torloisk was wooed so successfully by the married MacLean of Duart that she found herself in the family way, and in disgrace she was dismissed to the kitchen among the servants. Hearing about this, Duart's wife, who was childless, was so angry that she consulted a witch with the instruction to cast a spell that would postpone the birth indefinitely. Under the spell the poor girl was in misery, until one day a kindly passing packman, hearing her story, decided to help her if he could. So when during his rounds he arrived at Duart Castle, he casually mentioned that a son had been born to the kitchen girl at Torloisk when he knew he would be overheard by Lady MacLean. In a temper she stormed at the apparent failure of the witch's spell, tore a magic key out of its hiding place and threw it in the face of the witch. At that very moment the girl collapsed in the kitchen and gave birth to a fine boy, whose very first action was to grasp the handful of the straw which was all the bedding the other servants had time to provide. For that reason he was called Ailean na Sop - Allan of the Straws. The boy grew up to be a sturdy daring youngster. The old Torloisk laird died and his sole heir was the disgraced daughter, Shortly afterwards, she was married to a man whose sole ambition seemed to have been the take-over of the Torloisk estates, proving to be a cruel husband and vicious stepfather. On one occasion he even closed Allan's hands on some boiling food, burning his hands so badly that they were scarred for life.

Soon afterwards the boy left home to stay at a friendly place, where he grew to man's state, and entered into some reckless adventures that ended up by joining Danish pirates who even then staged an occasional raid on the Hebrides. Allan's initiative soon found him leader, with his own crew, of the raiding organisation, becoming feared throughout the Hebrides.

With his memory rather dimmed by the passing of time he decided to visit his old home in Torloisk, where, unknown to him, his mother had died some time before of abuse and a broken heart, and Allan's stepfather had achieved his ambition of being laird of Torloisk. When he saw Allan's little fleet anchoring in Loch Tuath off Torloisk the new laird was greatly alarmed, fearing that Allan had come at last to seek retribution, but Allan seemed to be reasonably friendly. This encouraged the crafty laird in his further ambition of seizing the island of Ulva from old MacQuarrie; so he hinted to Allen, as a prospective agent, that Ulva would be an excellent place to which he could retire and give up the sea. It would be easy to get rid of MacQuarrie.

At first this appealed to Allan, so he went over to Ulva with his men and confronted the old chief, who was quietly resigned. However, in the presence of this old family friend, Allan's memories began to come back, and when MacQuarrie quietly suggested that this take-over plan was unworthy of Allan, all his persecutions at the hands of his stepfather came back. He realised he had almost been made a tool of by the wicked man. Thinking, too, of the treatment to which he had learned his mother had been subjected, he returned to Torloisk, where he accused his stepfather, drew his sword and killed him on the spot. Allan then took over the chiefship of the MacLeans of Torloisk, gave up the sea, and retired and was married soon after. Allan has been wrongly credited with being the first chief of Torloisk, which is not the case. This story of half-truth and half folklore comes from the 17th century.

URRAIGH, AILEAN NA SOP

Although Ailean na Sop was now a reformed pirate, he never acquired the true character of a respectable gentleman. An example of this was told me by Seton Gordon, who had this little-known story from a former owner of Treshnish estate, Mr MacMorran.

Sometime after settling down in Torloisk Allan was entertaining MacNeill of Barra and his attractive daughter. A trip to the Treshnish Islands was arranged, and the party landed on Cairnburg Mor to examine the fortifications. When they were exploring the plateau top of the island, Allan, with same of his old piratical spirit, managed to isolate MacNeill's daughter, and quite near the edge of the 90ft cliff he began to pester the reluctant girl to such an unacceptable extent that one of her servants, who had happened to see what was going on, rushed up and pushed the unsuspecting Allan over the cliff! Luckily he landed on a shelf just below, from which, however, he could not climb back to the top without assistance. This the servant gave, but only on condition that Allan would leave the girl alone and never mention his presumptuous action.

This shelf is known as Urraigh Ailean na Sop, or Allan's Shelf. *Urraigh* is an obscure Gaelic word meaning an eyrie or shelf.

ULVA AND DR DAVID LIVINGSTONE

There is a connection between Dr Livingstone, the great missionary-explorer, and the island of Ulva, for his grandfather, a crofter, came from the island. He, in turn, was involved in the tragic affair of James of the Glen during the post-Culloden persecutions, one of the most blatant miscarriages of justice recorded in Scottish history. James Stewart, James of the Glen, was arrested for the murder of the so-called Red Fox, Campbell of Dunure, quite near when the Ballachulish Bridge now stands. James had been nowhere near the scene as was proved, and was even on friendly terms with Campbell, but being a Stewart, which was a clan hated by the Campbells, he was taken to Inveraray, and then, before a hostile Campbell jury, and even with Campbell of Argyll as judge, he was condemned to death by hanging and his body to be hung on gibbet on the bluff just above the south end of the bridge, under constant military guard. It hung there for three years, until the bones had to be wired up. Today, a cairn marks the site of the gibbet.

Local people were afraid to take some sort of action; but three Livingstone brothers living at Ballachulish could not stand the indignity any longer. When one of them enticed the soldier on guard down to the nearby hotel for a drink, the other two tore up the gibbet and reverently took the remains down to the boat they had left ready on the shore below, conveyed them out to an island, and buried them there temporarily. The hated gibbet was flung into the sea.

Anticipating inevitable punishment for their work the two brothers rowed down Loch Linnhe to Morvern, then crossing over to Mull they finally settled down as crofters in Ulva. I did not find out what happened to the third brother. One of the Ulva brothers drifted away. The other, Niall Mor, who had become a much respected man, also left the island, settling first in Glasgow, then in Blantyre. There his son Niall Bhig was born, who was to become the father of David Livingstone.

THE ENGLISH PIPER

There is another story involving Ulva. Beside the bridge over the River Aros at Salen, dominated by the ruined walls of Aros Castle, lies Dal na Sasunnach, the Field of the Englishman. This is where the prestigious Mull Agricultural Show is held every August, an event dating from 250 years ago.

In 1609 Lord Ochiltree sailed from Ayr with a small fleet to discipline the unruly clan chiefs in and around Mull. He induced the reluctant islanders to come on board the flagship by a ruse, lifted anchor and sailed away to the south, where the chiefs were sternly rebuked and released on promising to behave themselves. But that is by the way. When the ships departed so suddenly, an English soldier found himself left behind. He appears to have been an adaptable and likeable man who was accepted by the community, ending up as a shepherd in the 'tail' of MacArthur, who was a talented, inspired piper, who had been trained under the MacCrimmon of Boreraig, in Skye, who ran a piping school in Ulva. Amazingly, the Englishman discovered that he was a gifted and natural piper, and on a borrowed chanter he used to practice where no one would hear him, when he was tending MacArthur's sheep.

MacArthur was in the habit of practising his expert fingering behind his back on the stick he carried. When the Englishman was walking behind his master - as was his place - he picked up and memorised this on his chanter. Came the day when MacArthur, who had been practising for weeks, called a gathering of his critical friends and scholars to hear his fine rendering on the bagpipes of a very intricate air, "The Battle of the Birds." Just as he was about to walk forward and strike up the tune, the Englishman appeared playing the identical air on a borrowed set of bagpipes. Instead of the praise the poor man expected, he found to his horror he had committed a grave insult to his master before a highly critical audience. MacArthur's sons met him with a volley of abuse, drew their dirks and set upon him. In his ignorance and despair the poor man ran from the scene and made for the only spot to which his instincts led him, the place where he had landed in Aros Bay. There, in the Field of the Englishman, he was cornered and stabbed to death.

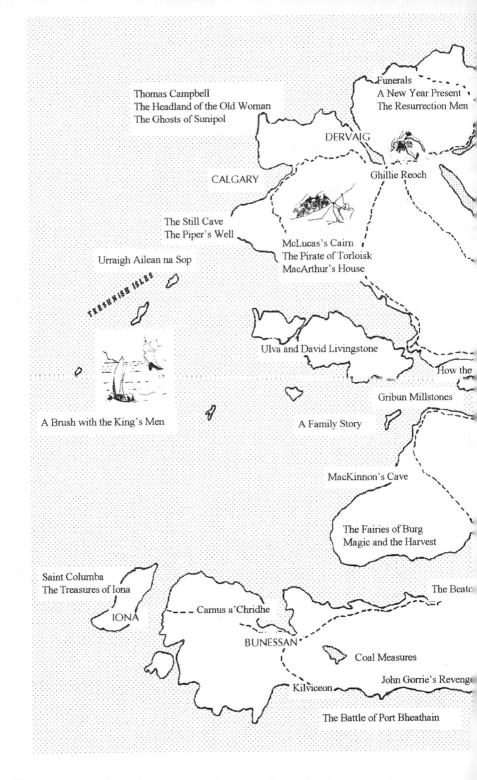

y Bay

OBERMORY

The Tobermory Galleon
The Skull

cal Monsters

CH FRISA

e Water-Horse   The English Piper

SALEN

ans Won a Battle

The Cailleach Bheur

Lady Rock

agedy Rock

LOCH BA   Murachadh Ghearr   CRAIGNURE

The Origin of
Clan Gillean

Clach Sguaban
The Headless Horseman

Glen More
The Dragon of Glen More   The Pedlar's Pool

rs

LOCHBUIE

The Herdsmen and
the Hanging Man

CARSAIG

The Nuns Cave

NORSE PLACE NAMES

In the passing, mention might be made of the influence of the Vikings on place names. Along the coasts the outstanding features bear names bestowed by the Norsemen as guiding points for their longboats; inland they are pure Gaelic. A combined example is Eas Fors, a waterfall that leaps for 90ft straight onto the beach near Ulva Ferry. Eas is Gaelic for a waterfall or cataract, so is Fors in the Norse. A double name for a single waterfall!

THE GRIBUN MILLSTONES

If you go for a few hundred yards west of the little ferry slip for Inch Kenneth, you will find a bed of hard grey sandstone just above high water mark. In it and partly finished there are a few millstones. Most lairds and large farms had a mill driven by the abundant water power and of course there was a demand for millstones. This mini-quarry was a source of stones, not only for Mull, but for such as Tiree, the 'Land of Corn', a fertile island worked by the monks of Iona. Boats could come right in at high tide and the finished stones could be rolled alongside with a temporary wooden axle that could be man-handled.

THE CAILLEACH BHEUR

This talented lady, the Hag of the Mountains, must have been one of those fabled monsters, or rather giantesses, who lived for all time. In her case she met her tragic death on the shore of Loch Ba. She lived within that enclosure of huge boulders located in the south-west of Mull known as Tota na Cailleach Bheur. She was so very old that her cattle once grazed on lands now either under the sea or eroded away. She must have survived the fires of the Tertiary Age. The Cailleach ranged widely. Do you know that it was through her carelessness that Loch Awe came into existence? You see, she had some favourite cows she grazed on Ben Cruachan which she watered daily from a well covered by a large flat stone. It was a magic well, for the cover could only be removed during daylight hours, and if left uncovered after that a vast deluge would pour out.

One hot sunny day she fell into such a sound sleep beside the well that darkness had just fallen when she woke up. The huge deluge had begun with a flood pouring down the Ben into the valley below. Before she could weave a spell that would allow her to replace the cover, such a volume of water had gushed out that it had filled the whole valley and that today is Loch Awe. She was so tall that the Sound of Mull barely came up to her knees. One time when she was returning to Mull with a big creel full of stones, a number fell out and formed the islands around Mull.

The poor Cailleach met her fate this way at Loch Ba. Her longevity depended on one thing. At intervals of 100 years, when she grew old like anybody else, she was obliged to immerse herself in the magic waters of Loch Ba in the early morning of her hundredth birthday, emerging once again as a handsome girl. This magic would end if she was unfortunate enough to hear the first note or cry of the day from bird or animal. Alas, on her final attempt, even as she was hobbling down to the water, she heard the distant bark of a restless dog (some say it was a cock that crew) and instead of being restored to youth, she fell, a lifeless old hag, on the shore in spite of a last desperate effort to reach the water.

THE FAIRIES OF BURG

Burg is the western extension of Ardmeanach in which lies 'The Wilderness' an area of fantastic rocks, caves, high cliffs and the famous Fossil Tree found by MacCulloch in 1819. The whole headland is haunted by the Little Folk, the fairy-type beings who could be induced to help you if approached in the proper manner and rewarded them at the finish.

There was this housewife who had gathered a great quantity of wool and was greatly troubled about the time it would take to process it on her spinning wheel. In fact, she was just about to invite all the neighbours to the customary communal work, when she remarked casually "Oh that the Little Folk would take pity on me and save all that work!" To her astonishment, hardly had she uttered those semi-jocular words than dozens of the Little People suddenly materialised in the room and set to work. Whenever they pronounced the name of each operation, it was done, and in no time at all the great pile of wool was ready for the making of clothes and weaving.

Such incidents were not uncommon, and the custom was to provide a hearty meal for the fairy-people. However, this woman was quite unprepared, with little food to spare, and as the expectant fairies sat down around the room, she cried "Oh, my sorrow; look, my larder has nothing but some oatmeal and a few eggs." "That will do," they cried, and when the woman began to prepare a meal, however much she used up, there was plenty more. When they had finished the fairy *sluagh* simply vanished. Another woman was not so lucky much the same happened - no food in the house; but the wee folk kept sitting and sitting until the woman was distraught, and slipped out of the house to seek the advice of a wise old woman next door. "What you will do," she said, "is to rush back pretending to be most excited, and shout 'Burg is on fire! Burg is on fire!'" Suddenly distressed and panic-stricken her guests began to call out - "My home, my little ones!" and vanished for good, forgetting to undo the good work they had done for no reward. However, she never again saw a single member of the fairy host.

MAGIC AND THE HARVEST

Somewhere over near Burg a farmer had been obliged to sack two of his workers about harvest time. One day, when the corn was standing in stooks after scything, a stranger came up and very civilly asked the farmer if he might have a few stooks. To this the kindly farmer readily agreed, so the stranger produced a piece of rope and laid it along the ground. He placed a sheaf on it; and another, and another, and the more he added, the more space was left for more sheaves, until the bewildered farmer saw every sheaf of corn gone and his harvest ruined.

He was a religious man, and in his despair he called on Providence to help him. Hardly had he uttered his prayer than when he looked up, there was every single stook back in its place! The two disgruntled servants he had dismissed for incompetence had tried to get their own back by seeking the services of a man who dabbled in witchcraft, but that was undone by the intervention of Providence.

HOW THE MACLEANS WON A BATTLE

It was along the south shore of Loch na Keal that MacLean's little army was saved from slaughter by the ingenuity of a wily MacLean sympathiser in the opposing force. A massive and quite unexpected fleet of galleys with a strong force of MacDonalds and their allies landed a formidable array of fighting men on the south shore of Loch na Keal to ravage the lands of Duart. Such clan fights resembled a duel; a truce was declared until the opposing forces had agreed a time and place for the confrontation. This allowed the MacLeans time to gather together enough of their men to put up at least a token resistance. On the morning of the appointed day a wily MacLean sympathiser, a spy, as it were, in the invading force, with some official post, assumed such an air of apprehension that MacDonald himself asked the man what ailed him? Was he afraid of being killed? The officer replied gloomily that what was troubling him was a dream he had had the night before in which he was warned by a supernatural being that MacDonald's force would be driven back to the galleys with great slaughter. MacDonald was greatly impressed. Such visions from the supernatural were taken seriously in those days. He gave orders for his force to break camp, return to the galleys, and seek a more advantageous site for the invasion. Seeing his opponents retiring in some apparent disorder, Duart and his men descended on them and created such a slaughter that the invaders were glad to escape and give up their plans. Concocted as the dream was, the outcome was prophesied!

GLEN MORE

Surely in all Scotland there is no other glen with such a store of folklore and superstition. This barren, lonesome glen, hemmed in by high hills, where no trees grow; where telegraph poles used to be uprooted by the wild winds from Loch Scridain, could hardly fail to inflame the imaginations of people long ago. The stories will bear this out - with a touch of facts thrown in.

THE DRAGON OF GLEN MORE

This story was told to me by the late Seton Gordon. Long, long ago the glen was terrorised by a great fierce dragon whose lair was on the top of Cnoc Fhada, above Loch Sguabain, where you can still see the hollow worn by its scaly body. Livestock vanished down its hungry maw, so, too, did anyone foolish enough to venture into the glen. The local king was in despair and finally offered half his kingdom and the hand of his particularly lovely daughter to anyone who would rid him of this importunate beast.

Handsome warriors in armour from head to toe, with all the latest weapons, confronted the dragon, but vanished like all the others. At last nobody would venture within miles of the place. However, one day a young man who had spent his last groat on the venture arrived by ship and anchored off Kinloch, at the head of Loch Scridain. He landed a herd of sub-standard cattle and set about laying a floating causeway of big casks between ship and shore, into which he drove long sharp spikes. Then armed with only his sgian dubh, which he required to urge on the reluctant cattle, he headed away up the glen. Up on Cnoc Fhada the dragon smacked its chops in anticipation when it spied the cattle coming over the watershed from Craig, remarking to itself - "They'll never learn!" So it came bounding down breathing fire and smoke. As soon as he saw it, the young man immediately turned the now willing herd back to Loch Scridain, but the dragon overtook with ease. When its hot breath was felt, the young man quickly slaughtered one of the herd. The eating of it delayed the greedy beast; then it took up the pursuit. Well, this action was repeated all the way back to the ship; when the dragon was about to overtake, another poor cow was sacrificed, until by the time the herd reached the end of the causeway only one poor old cattle-beast was left. The slaughter of this one gave the young man just time to dodge out to the ship between the spikes. Enraged at seeing the last of its prey escaping, the dragon began to crawl along the line of casks: but first one spike, then another caught it up, and the more the beast struggled, the harder it became impaled until at last it lay helpless, grinding its teeth and emitting only a thin trickle of smoke. Borrowing a cutlass, the young hero strolled out and chopped off its head.

Triumphantly he upped the ship's anchor, and towing behind it the line of casks with the evidence of the dead dragon he sailed round to the Port of the King. There, this ingenious young man claimed the reward. Such a clever man was an instant success with the king, and he and the princess hit it off well.

CLACH SGUABAIN

A more credible story from Glen More concerns the disharmony between two of the
Fingalian giants, Nicol and Sguabain. Nicol was standing over at Loch Spelve,
while Sguabain was in Glen More above the loch that bears his name. Being giants,
of course, they could see each other across Cnoc Fhada and the intervening hills.
This day they were holding a discussion that became so heated that they lost their
tempers. Sguabain tore up a boulder and hurled it angrily at Nicol. Not to be
outdone, Nicol picked up a great pointed rock and threw it at Sguabain. If you
do not believe this, halt on the new road above Loch Sguabain and walk down a few
yards to a passing place in the old road below, at the edge of which you will see
Clach Sguabain, the stone thrown by Nicol that landed beside Sguabain.
Apparently, with equally poor aim, Sguabain's boulder lies on the shore of Loch
Spelve beside where Nicol was standing.

THE HEADLESS HORSEMAN

Still another story from Glen More combines a touch of folklore and superstition with authentic history. I became aware of the existence of the awful spectre of the headless horseman who haunts Mull roads after dusk when I was still a schoolboy with two lonely miles of road between home and school to walk summer and winter. One morning I learned that the grocer's van had been confronted by the ghost the previous evening at a nasty bend of the road, escaping by cutting right across on the heathery flat and avoiding the spectre. Why, I saw the evidence of that in the deep tyre marks on the soft ground with my own eyes!

When I began to take an interest in the subject, I found another and much earlier piece of evidence. There were two very old trees still growing, one beside the Salen/Gruline road that was taken away when the road was widened, the other, still there, beside the bridle path that skirts Loch Ba on its way over Mam Clachaig to Glen More. In each case a MacLean of Duart who was walking along in the dusk was attacked by the headless horseman, but by gripping a sapling with one hand to steady himself, he fended off his adversary with the other hand until the cock crew, when, of course, ghosts have to retire. However, the struggle had been so violent that the two saplings were almost torn out by the roots and grew horizontally ever since. I'll now explain why the ghost had a particular animosity against MacLeans.

The apparition was in fact the ghost of Eoghann a'Chinn Bhig, Ewen of the Little Head, who was the only son of John, the aged 5th chief of the MacLaines of Lochbuie. The following event took place in the year 1538. Ewen's home lay on the little islet at the east end of Loch Sguabain, where the stonework can still be traced, a natural defensive position. Lochbuie and Moy Castle lay a few miles through a glen to the south of the three lochs, of which Loch Sguabain is the most easterly. Now, Ewen was married to a greedy and ambitious daughter of MacDougall of Lorne. Not satisfied with the grant of the lands of Morvern, she nagged Ewen to ask his father for more and more concessions, until the old man declared that enough was enough. Ewen still pestered him, but his father was adamant. Nagged on by his wife, he put aside filial duty and threatened his father that he would take what he wished by force. Tempers flared and armed confrontation became unavoidable. It was agreed formally to meet at an agreed place and fight it out. I have never been able to trace the exact location of the fight, except that is described as a "grassy lawn, where the bones of dead men have been found." Some say it took place near Craig, four miles to the west, others at Blar Cheann a'Chnocain, about the watershed of Glen More. I prefer the alternative as being much more likely: that it took place on the boggy flat nearer where the River Lussa emerges from Loch Sguabain.

The day before the fight, Ewen had an ominous meeting with a fairy woman. Riding his black charger, as the story goes, he came across this fairy washing blood-stained garments beside a small burn. With great respect, as is due to the Little People, he asked her if she could prophesy the outcome of tomorrow's fight. She gave him a strange reply: "If you find no butter on the table in the morning, and have to ask for it, the fight will go badly for you."

In the flurry of preparations Ewen forgot all about the prophecy until he found no butter on the table and had to ask for it to be brought. Although now filled with apprehension, he marshalled his followers and faced up to his father's, among whom was the wily and far-sighted Maclean of Duart, brother of Lochbuie. There was a desperate fight, but Ewen's father's superior numbers began to prevail - thanks to the MacLean men (no wonder the headless Horseman hated the Duart MacLeans). Seeing his men so sorely pressed, Ewen bravely charged into the middle of the fight, laying himself open to attack by the opposing foemen. A Duart man took a great swipe at him with a claymore and completely severed his head from his body. Jammed in the stirrups of his maddened horse his headless body was carried to where a footbridge replaces the former ford over the Lussa, just above the Falls of Lussa and below the lowest ruined building of Torness. At the top of the steep bank across the river the horse came to a stop exhausted and the body of Eoghann a'Chinn Bhig fell to the ground. At this spot his followers set up a tiny marking cairn and interred the body for a day or two before bringing it back to the home in Loch Sguabain. It is said that when Ewen's favourite hunting hound saw the headless body of its master, every hair fell off its body! Ever since then, the ghost of Ewen haunts the Mull roads after dusk, mounted on his ghostly horse. He is said to have galloped furiously round Moy Castle when a death in the MacLaine family was imminent. His chief target is a MacLean of Duart for the treacherous support given by that clan to his father. A versatile ghost, said even to fly over to Coll, where a branch of the MacLeans held sway. There is a sequel to the story of Eoghann a'Chinn Bhig which I shall tell you later.

I had often been told about the existence of the tiny cairn above the Falls of Lussa, but no-one could tell me the exact spot, until I asked Seton Gordon, that great authority in Celtic lore. He told me that as far as he knew, only the carrier from Fionnphort and himself knew the location, and he gave me directions. My family and I explored the locality for an hour in company with Mr David James, the then owner of the estate of Torosay, and success! There in the exact spot, deeply hidden in the heather, was the mossy little cairn, just beside the path leading to the Falls and about 150 yards below Torness. Subsequently we added a stone every time we passed along the adjacent fine new road.

MURACHADH GEARR

After the death of Eoghann a'Chinn Bhig, only son and heir to Lochbuie, John, the chief, was left without an heir - and this is where the forethought of his brother, MacLean of Duart, paid off for having supported him. Without warning, Duart seized John, Moy Castle, and all Lochbuie, sending John far away to the security of the lonely prison house on Cairnburg Mor, in the Treshnish Islands, where the ruins still stand. His only company was a housekeeper, though boatmen were sent regularly to replenish the provisions.

After two years, the boatmen returning from a visit reported that the housekeeper seemed as if she was about to become a mother. This alarmed Duart, for an illegitimate son could legally claim an inheritance in those days - in this case the lost lands and castle of Lochbuie. At once Duart appointed a doctor and nurse to attend to the birth, and moved the housekeeper conveniently to the mainland of Mull. The doctor was instructed that if a boy-child was born, he was to be put to death.

However, when the time came, twins were born, a boy and a girl. The doctor, who had been absent at the time, was handed the little girl, so all was well and he reported accordingly to the relief of Duart. The nurse, who had attended the birth, hid the little boy and secretly had him conveyed to a foster-mother at the MacGillivrays in Glen Cannel. Here he grew up, receiving his early training, becoming a skilled fighting man with a deep-seated hatred of Duart's treachery.

In Gaelic, the boy was known as Murachadh Gearr, short or dumpy Murdoch, because of his stocky appearance. Reaching manhood, he set off to see the world that lay beyond Glencannel, finishing up as a guest of the Earl of Antrim over in Ireland, who extended to him the traditional hospitality of a year and a day. Murdoch confided his life story and hopes of reclaiming his inheritance to the Earl, who promised him every assistance.

In early summer Murdoch, with only the twelve companions he requested, sailed over from Ireland, knowing that if he landed safely he was sure to have the Lochbuie clansmen at his back. They climbed a high cliff and made their way unseen to the precincts of Moy Castle, hoping to capture it in the night when the watchers became careless. However, hidden as he was, Murdoch dislodged a stone which started a small avalanche that startled a woman down below who was milking a cow, who exclaimed what seemed to be a stock phrase "God be with you Murdoch!" Murdoch revealed himself, and asked the woman what she meant. Sadly, she explained that she referred to her absent foster-son who had left Glencannel long ago. With joy, Murdoch recognised and was recognised by his own foster-mother. He told her of his ambitions to take the castle and reclaim his inheritance and asked her if she had any helpful ideas. She advised him to wait until the garrison was asleep; then to go to the nearby enclosures where just that day the calves had been separated from their mothers. Open the gates, she said and the cows and calves will run bellowing to find each other, raising such a commotion that the men would come running out of the castle to restore order. Station yourselves on each side of the door, she said, and as each man comes out, strike him down. Thoughtful, Murdoch asked, "what if your husband is among them?" To which she replied in what has become a Gaelic saying, "Let the tail go with the hide!" Everything happened exactly as planned and Murdoch was master of the castle. Duart's son and his wife had slept through it all upstairs, but Murdoch generously left them alone until morning, when he broke the news to them and allowed Duart's son to depart and carry the bad news to his father.

As expected, the clansmen flocked to Murdoch's aid and a great confrontation was threatened between Duart and himself. Murdoch attempted to seize Aros castle, but it was too strongly defended, and the two sides met on opposite sides of the river near Aros Bridge. In the night, when the men slept and the guards drowsed, Murdoch and his faithful Irish friend MacCormick crossed the river, and evading the sentries, came to where his uncle Duart was lying sleeping with his sword beside him. Gently removing the weapon, Murdoch placed his own distinctive sword beside the sleeping figure and safely returned to his own side of the river. Next morning, when Duart became aware of the exchange of swords and realised how his life had been spared by his nephew, he was greatly touched. He contacted Murdoch and established what was to become a lifetime's friendship.

Thus did Murachadh Gearr regain the lost lands of Lochbuie and became the 6th chief, dying in 1586. He generously provided for his helpful foster-mother, and in the case of MacCormick, who had been such a faithful friend, he directed that Moy Castle was to be open house to anyone of that name. In fact, above the doorway of Moy there are still traces of where a stone lintel was once in place above the door, bearing the carving in Gaelic, 'Food and drink to MacCormick.'

JOHN GORRIE'S REVENGE

One day a chief of Lochbuie organised a great deer hunt and appointed John Gorrie to take up a position where he could prevent the driven deer from escaping through a narrow pass. However, there was such a sudden stampede of frightened deer that he was quite powerless to turn them, and the hunt was almost a failure.
Lochbuie was so angry at what he thought was Gorrie's neglect that he ordered him to be tied up and severely punished. The punishment was the cruel one of emasculation, which was carried out on a cliff top west of Carsaig Bay, near the Carsaig Arches. When the agonised man was released he darted forward, seized the

chief's son and leaped over the cliff, landing on a narrow shelf below - something like Ailean na Sop. The anguished father stood above promising Gorrie anything if he would just allow his son to be rescued. Gorrie responded that he would do so if the chief submitted to the same indignity as he had suffered. The chief loved his son so much that he agreed but when Gorrie was satisfied that the act had been carried out he grasped the child and leaped with him to their deaths on the rocks below. Ever since, this hill-edge has been known as Gorrie's Leap.

THE BEATON DOCTORS

Just beyond the Free Church at Pennyghael and to the right-hand side of the road as you go towards Iona, you will see a simple but substantial cairn surmounted by a stone cross. This was built many years ago to perpetuate the memory of the famous doctors, the Ollamh Muileach, a family of Beatons who came originally from Béthune in France, hence the name.

They were hereditary physicians to first the Lords of the Isles, then to the MacLeans of Duart. In fact, they conducted an informal medical service throughout the area. Little is known now of those famous medical men, one of whom was exceptionally skilled in the use of herbs. In fact the enclosure beyond Pennyghael where the herbs were raised could be traced early this century. In Campbell's *West Highland Tales* three brothers are mentioned, John, who was the chief practitioner in Mull, whose tomb is in Iona; Fergus specialised in Islay, while Gilleadh was the herbalist. Reports of John's skill even reached Edinburgh and came to the ears of the king, who invited him to attend a meeting where the best doctors in Scotland were to be tested. It is a long story; but to be brief, the king feigned an illness which the doctors were to identify and suggest a remedy. All of them took it very seriously except Dr Beaton, who was not afraid to call the king's bluff. This so impressed the king that he had no hesitation in declaring Beaton the best in Scotland. On his way back to Mull, John was poisoned by his jealous rivals who slipped poison into his food, and with a healthy respect for his skill first took the precaution of removing every possible antidote for which John could have called.

There are many imaginative stories told about the Beaton doctors. The very first Beaton, so it was said, was a young man who was assisting a skilled Irish doctor. By certain magical processes involving a white snake and a hazel stick brought from Mull, he found himself transformed into a skilled medical practitioner the moment a drop of the potion in which the unfortunate snake was being brewed fell accidentally on his hand. Then there was the time he saved the life of a chief of Lochbuie suffering from an inoperable throat abcess. He prepared in the presence of the chief an unmentionably loathsome infusion which friends were invited to taste. The expressions on their faces were so laughter-provoking that the chief, in a fit of mirth, so strained his throat that the abcess broke up and saved his life. Only once was the doctor baffled when his own daughter fell ill and died in spite of all his medical skill. A post-mortem was held, and it was found that the death was attributable to the presence of a live frog in her stomach. The frog was kept alive and fed different foods in an effort to find a treatment for any such future illness. One day they fed the frog nettle soup, and the frog died. John was distraught that he had not thought to administer such a simple cure.

He was able to save the life of another girl who had swallowed a tadpole that had grown into a frog. In some way he diagnosed ʿ ɾ condition by the tone of her singing and cured her with a plate of nettle soup. And so on . . . On a squared stone in the face of the Beaton cairn you might be able to trace the much eroded inscription - GMB 1582 DMB, said to be the initials of the leading Beaton doctors.

COAL MEASURES

You might say that Mull is an unlikely place to find coal, but in a few places there are thin seams of rather poor coal or lignite: at Ardtun but rather more definite, just south-west of Carsaig, on the western slopes of Ben an Aoinaidh. Here in 'Coal Burn' there is a seam of three feet or so of poor but burnable quality. A measure of this coal was part of the rental paid for the farm of Shiaba nearby, and the blacksmith at Pennyghael used it in his smithy after conveying it over the rough old track that can still be traced in places.

KILVICEON

This cell or chapel of Ewen lies to the west of Shiaba. Its substantial stonework and the use of shell lime as mortar point to its antiquity, perhaps as long ago as the days of St Columba. The stones were prepared at the seashore at mile distant and passed from hand to hand along a line of volunteer helpers until delivered at the feet of the masons.

THE BATTLE OF PORT BHEATHAIN

Many Iron Age duns or forts line the south coast of the Ross of Mull, which would have been a natural point of attack for sea raiders who were probably later militant colonists from Ireland seeking new lands later to be established as the kingdom of Dalriada in Argyll and the west, a nucleus of the Scots. Some of Mull's coastal forts were useful defence positions in the days of the Vikings, even having their use as late as times of clan troubles, for instance Dun nan Gheird, which stands above Port Bheathain was used as a look-out post and gave first warnings of what was to develop into a fight between the MacLeans and the MacPhees of Colonsay.   It all started with the murder of a MacGillivray of Glencannel, a family friendly with the chief of the MacLeans. This was carried out by a renegade MacLean, who boasted of his deed as he fled through the Ross of Mull, found an unattended boat and rowed south to Colonsay to seek protection from MacPhee of Colonsay, between whom and Duart there was bad blood. Learning of the escape of the murderer, Duart sent a message to Colonsay requesting the execution of the culprit and the return of his head to Duart.

MacPhee did indeed attend to the execution of the MacLean renegade; but sent his head back with the indignity of a twig being run through the eye sockets as a carrying handle. This Duart regarded as an intolerable insult and a furious row broke out that could only be settled in blood, such was the pride of clan chiefs at even the hint of an insult. Lookouts on Dun nan Gheird saw in the distance a great fleet of galleys filled with fighting men approaching from Colonsay. At once Duart called up his own men with signal fires spreading the warning throughout Mull. His force gathered not far from Port Bheathain, sufficient, he thought, to overcome the MacPhees. However, he took no chances, but adopted the cunning tactic of dividing his force into two sections, one to hide in ambush behind a little hill while the other put up a token resistance to draw the opponents into the ambush. All went as planned; when the opponents had triumphantly driven off the MacLeans as they thought, they received a massive attack on their exposed flank and rear. The routed MacPhees were slaughtered as they retired in disorder to their galleys, and especially at the waterside when they were boarding their galleys.

CAMUS A'CHRIDHE

The story connected with this lovely little bay in the Ross of Mull - the Bay of the Heart - is of more classical than Celtic imagery.

Fraoch was in love with a beautiful maiden, but of all things, her mother was a jealous rival, although secretly, for his affections! Rather than see her daughter the chosen one, she resolved to kill Fraoch. She pretended to have a serious illness whose cure was the juice from rowan berries plucked from a tree growing on an off-shore islet, guarded by a fierce monster. Anxious to please his future mother-in-law Fraoch swam out and came very cautiously to the rowan tree, from which he plucked the necessary berries beside the sleeping monster, which awoke from sleep as the young man was retiring and gave chase. Nimbly avoiding it, Fraoch started to swim for the sandy shore, with the monster gaining on him. They met on the shore where Fraoch fought desperately and although he was killed by the monster, the fight ended with its heart grasped in Fraoch's hand. Fraoch's betrothed, when she came searching for him was overcome by the horrid sight of the monster and Fraoch lying dead and expired on the sand beside him.

SAINT COLUMBA

Many stories have come down from St Columba after his 6th century landing in Iona as a devout militant missionary who would stand no nonsense. His life and works need no description. In Iona, however, he found that he did not have things all his own way, thanks to the lingering influence left in what is sometimes called Druids' Island. For instance, the incident involving his friend Oran, whose well-preserved chapel stands beside Iona abbey, in the cemetery called after him - Reilig Odhrain. This was the traditional burying place for many kings of Scotland.

Try as they would, the workers could not complete the building of Oran's chapel, whose walls fell down as fast as rebuilt. In the end St Columba had to resort to a sad pagan sacrifice to have the pagan influence removed; that was, to bury some live person beneath the foundations. A volunteer was asked for, and at once Oran offered, and they buried him with great reluctance, for he was a particular friend of St Columba, and the work went on unchecked. St. Columba was anxious to have one final look at his friend, so he ordered his face to be uncovered. When the last spadeful was removed and Oran's face exposed, he uttered the terrible words - "Heaven is not as described, and Hell ... wasn't too bad." This so shocked St Columba that he hastily ordered - "Earth, earth in the mouth of Oran that he blab no more!" - and he was hastily covered up. Yes, the memory of the old gods remains in the hill Dun Manannan, after the god of the sea.

To hear some of the old stories, one might think Columba had been around a century ago. At Salen, for instance, you will see a low rocky bluff in the middle of the village from which he is said to have delivered a sermon - and "not very well attended" as you will hear the local story. On Iona of course you will see by contrast Sithean Mor, the big Fairy Knowe, where St Columba was known to have communed with the angels. Called Angels' Knowe today.

The Saint is said to have refused to allow a woman or a cow to be seen on Iona, and there is the ancient Gaelic poem which translated means "Where there is a cow there is a woman; and where there is a woman there is mischief." He also banned frogs and snakes from the island.

It was in the 12th century that women really gained an official foothold when Reginald, Lord of the Isles, sponsored a nunnery for the Black Nuns. Just north of Fionnphort, below the granite quarries, there is a fine little bay protected by the off-shore island of Eilean nam Ban - Womens' Island. Here there are the outlines of old habitations where the womenfolk connected with Iona - the wives and relatives of the secular workers were said to have been housed.

THE TREASURES OF IONA

During the Reformation Iona was sacked and turned into what has been described as a sacred desert by the bigoted Reformers, acting with the full authority of the Scottish parliament. Irreplaceable historical treasures dating back to the days of St Columba were ruthlessly destroyed along with the buildings. Fleeing monks carried with them whatever they could, items which ended up in the archives of Paris and other European centres. Fortunately the wonderful Book of Kells had been sent to Ireland in good time. Certain items are supposed to have been hidden on the Treshnish fortress-island of Cairnburg Mor but discovered and destroyed by Cromwell's men.

FUNERALS

Funerals in Mull used to be highly formalised; they could even be much of a social occasion. Even the poorest crofter would be prepared to sell a cattle beast, or even a horse, to provide a seemly funeral for a dead relative. Drink was essential, although sometimes over-indulgence led to family disputes, even at the graveside. Furthermore, there were a few occasions when the coffin was being conveyed by horse and cart, and on arrival at the cemetery it was found to have slipped off the open back of the cart on some steep hill and the shame-faced mourners had to go back and retrieve it. There were no official grave diggers, so the relatives had to dig the grave themselves. I remember hearing of one incident when a young relative was deep in the digging he stooped and lifted a skull. Proudly displaying it to the mourners round the graveside, he remarked, "This will be my grandfather. Man, had he no' a grand set of teeth!"

Interments were often held at distant cemeteries, such as over at Kilmore, in Dervaig, an eight-mile walk for a cortège if no conveyance was available. Members took it in turn to relieve the men holding the 'bearers' on which the coffin rested, and periodically a halt was called for a rest. Often, on departing, each mourner left a stone to form a tiny cairn where the coffin had rested - you will see a number of those practically hidden just beside the fourth milestone on the Tobermory/Dervaig road.

This associating stones with the dead is a strange tradition, for pebbles have been found beside and with interments in the crypt of Iona Abbey. It is possible that this is a tenuous memory from very long ago when mourners placed stones to ward off scavenging animals, the origin now forgotten and replaced by a traditional gesture. There was a curious custom observed at times; everyone met on the road by the cortège was expected to drink 'To the health of the corpse' from the communal bottle!

My father once had a most disturbing experience from which he returned home visibly shaken. I remember well how he described it although I was just a boy.

He nad gone for a walk with a Tobermory friend for a mile or two up the road to Dervaig. Just as they were about the second milestone, his friend hastily removed his cap, caught my father by the arm and drew him in to the side of the road with his eyes moving to follow what my father could not see, and whispered - "Don't you see them? It's the funeral of old ----------- from Tobermory on the way to Kilmore." Presently he donned his cap again and their walk was resumed.

Now, at the time of the vision, old --------- in Tobermory was very much alive, but he died very suddenly a fortnight later and his funeral passed the place of the vision at exactly the same time of day. Such inexplicable instances of 'Second Sight' were not uncommon, and it is hard to disbelieve or discredit them.

THE RESURRECTION MEN

Do you know that body snatchers - the Resurrection Men - were to be found even in the Hebrides? In the Isle of Mull my father used to describe that when he was a young man - that would be in the 1870s - he made up a party of grave watchers in Pennygown cemetery near Salen, where there had been an interment. They were there on watch for a fortnight, with a tarpaulin for shelter and a big fire of driftwood from the nearby shore. A Tobermory man told me an authentic story about the old cemetery in Tobermory. Here, at the topside of the cemetery, beside the boundary wall, you will see a damaged recumbent tombstone with a tiny hole punched through the centre. This, my friend told me, was caused by a slug fired by the watchers at two body snatchers during the night following an interment. His grandfather, he added, broke his leg between two tombstones when the party chased after the two disciples of Jerry Cruncher.

The receiver of bodies in Tobermory was said to be a local doctor, a bachelor, who lived at the outskirts of the town. He securely packed bodies brought to him in casks of brine, to be conveyed unsuspected by cargo ship to the Broomielaw in Glasgow, where they were collected by the Medical School whose Anatomy Class was always short of material. The going rate paid by the doctor was £5 for a nice fresh corpse, a lot of money in those days. The nefarious work of this doctor was finally proved and sharply ended by a small group of the lads of the village.

One day, a sailing ship dropped anchor in the Bay and the crew came ashore to enjoy a refreshment at the bars of the local hotels. The village men were in one of them, when a big Negro from the ship came walking in and they struck up a conversation with him over a drink or two, for he was a jolly, friendly type. After a while, a brilliant idea occurred to the party, which they discussed and then explained to the Negro, asking if he would co-operate, which he did with delight.

There had been an interment in the cemetery the day before, which made the plan logical and acceptable. So late that night, a knock came to the back door of the doctor's house. With lighted candle, he opened it and saw the dark figures with the familiar canvas-wrapped object on the ground at their feet. Although he was not expecting a delivery, the doctor, although surprised, slipped a five-pound note into the outstretched hands of the waiting party, which melted wordlessly into the darkness.

Setting down the flickering candle, the doctor dragged the long bundle into the kitchen and decided to check the quality of his purchase. But as he bent over it, the canvas seemed to move in the flickering shadows and as he bent even closer a gleaming knife-blade began to slice the bundle open and a huge, grinning black face with flashing teeth began to rise up, flourishing a long knife.

They say the doctor finished cowering under the bed of a douce church elder and his wife at the other side of the village, and that ended the practice of body-snatching in Tobermory. Above the wall behind the medico's house, the young men who had been joined by the co-operative Negro, were rolling about in hysterical laughter. Not only did they have such fun, but they were further in funds to the extent of a £5 note, which would go far to celebrate their achievement!

THE THREE LEAPS OF THE GHILLIE REOCH

This man, the Red Fellow, was a MacKinnon of Mishnish, in the days before the clan was ousted to its headquarters in Skye. He was a great athlete and an expert swordsman. One day, when he was walking through the boggy hollow that lies below a passing place on the present road between Achnadrish and Dervaig, just over the watershed, he was ambushed by a party of raiding MacLeans over from Coll, intent on paying off old scores. However, they were facing this expert swordsman, who kept beating off their attacks.

Numbers were beginning to prevail and, in order to prevent himself from being surrounded, he took the first of his great leaps, 30 feet from a standing start. Again hemmed in, he repeated his performance with a similar leap of 30 feet which, however, was hardly enough to free him from pressure, so he baffled his attackers by taking a final leap of 45 feet and backwards at that to his starting point.

This elusive performance so angered the chief of the raiding party, that he hurled his sword in a temper at the Ghillie Reoch who, of course, evaded it easily and seeing his opponent left without a weapon, he darted in and ran him through the body. This was too much for the raiders, who gave up the attack and retired to their galley at Mᶦ ɪgary, carrying the body of their leader. Three small cairns mark the spots from which the MacKinnon took off on his gigantic leaps. I have measured the exact distance between them.

THE HERDSMEN AND THE HANGING MAN

This story dates from the 16th or 17th centuries when clan chiefs still had the power of Pit and Gallows, summary justice by execution. It was told me by an old friend in Mull and a fine Gaelic speaker - gone, sadly, long since. Of course translated into the poor medium of the English it loses much of the asides that would have delighted a ceilidh round the fireside.

Eachann (Hector) and Seumas (James) were two herdsmen who looked after the black cattle of the chief of Lochbuie, animals in which lay the wealth of the clan folks. One day Bean Eachann (Hector's wife) looked in to see her neighbour, Bean Seumas (James's wife) whom she found stirring a pot over the fire.

"And what have you making in the pot today?" she asked.

"Oh, just a drop of brochan for Seumas."

"And what kind of a broth is it?"

"Ach, it's just some dubh brochan" - a simple broth with water and oatmeal.

"My is Seumas not the poor man!" commented Bean Eachann, "Can you no' get a piece of meat to put in the brochan? Why, every year Lochbuie gives Eachann a whole ox for himself, and we are never without a bit of salt beef in the house." She paused for a minute and added very confidentially, "I'll tell you what we will do. I'll send Eachann over tonight and he can plan with Seumas how to get an ox. The chief will never miss it."

So that night the two men met and put their heads together and discussed how to steal an ox. Said Eachann, "We daren't ask himself for one because he is a hard man; but this is what we will do. If they miss one of the beasts and ask us, we won't be telling a lie; you Seumas will do the lifting and bring it over to me to hide. You can swear 'I didn't take it home' and I will say, 'I didn't take it from the fold' and that will be true enough."

So, the very next night when everything was quiet, Eachann made his way round the edge of the wood that grew beside the cattle enclosure, where he lit a small fire as a signal to Seumas that the coast was clear. But as Seumas crept quietly and a little fearfully down to the enclosure, he was sure he heard men talking not far off and a dog barking, so he hid and waited for a long, long time. After a while, he decided to slip right through the wood and tell Eachann they should put the whole plan off until another time.

Now that very evening, Lochbuie was entertaining a party of friends in the castle. He was describing how he had ordered a thief to be hanged in the wood beside the castle. The *uisge beatha* had been flowing freely, encouraging the boaster and fortifying the timid. One of the guests spoke up and laid a friendly wager with the chief that he hadn't a man in his 'tail' who would venture into the wood in the dark and come back to the castle with a *brog* (shoe) from the hanged man. There was a long silence until it was broken by big MacDonald, the head boatman who, when the wager was explained to him, got up and swore he would do the deed.

Now Seumas had still been in hiding when the bold MacDonald came into the wood, at the other side of which Eachann was sitting by the fire awaiting the arrival of Seumas, and all unconscious of the dreadful figure hanging at the end of a rope just a few yards into the wood beside him.

By a coincidence, both Eachann and the corpse were big men, with bushy red beards, so when MacDonald just missed seeing his objective, the hanging thief, he carried on to investigate the small fire at the edge of the wood and there, beside it, he saw to his horror what he assumed to be the red-bearded corpse warming himself before a fire. This was too much. Panic-stricken, he started back in fear and fled back to the castle, where he stammered out a description of the unearthly apparition he had seen. His audience was quite unimpressed.

"Just as I said!" crowed the man who had wagered the chief. "A lot of cowards you have, Lochbuie," and the chief lowered his disappointment. At that, however, a crippled servant boasted to the others - "A fine lot you are! If only I had my feet under me, I would come back with the leg as well as the brog."

This boast restored some of MacDonald's confidence, so he challenged the cripple: "Come on then and I will put a good pair of feet under you," so the cripple was left with no option: and off they went with the cripple on MacDonald's back, But when the boaster saw the same dreadful apparition sitting by the fire he was panic-stricken and struggled to get off. But MacDonald , although equally scared, held on to him and stood his ground.   Just then Eachann, waiting patiently for the cautious Seumas, saw the dim figure of MacDonald at the edge of the wood. Thinking it was Seumas returning with the ox, he stood up and called softly - "And have you come back?"
"Yes," stammered the scared MacDonald.
"And have you got him?"
"Yes."
"And is he fat?"- but this was too much for MacDonald, "Fat or thin, here he is . ." and throwing the cripple towards the dreadful figure he took to his heels as if the Evil One was behind him, with the terrified cripple hopping and crawling behind him on his hands and knees.

Meantime, Eachann, thinking they might be watchers sent by the chief to hurry back and report, thought he might as well forget about Seumas in all this mix-up, go to the castle and make a full and frank appeal for mercy. When MacDonald rushed terrified into the castle, they said, "Well, and did you get the shoe this time?"

"Indeed and I did not," he cried; "The hanged man was still sitting at the fire. He must have been hungry, for he asked me if the cripple was fat, so I threw him at the man and came back. By now the cripple will be eaten!" But as he spoke there was uproar as the poor exhausted cripple came clawing his way in, screaming that the corpse was at his heels. It was a changed atmosphere within the castle. The door was locked and barred against the powers of evil, and everyone rushed to arm himself: so when Eachann came to the door he had to knock and wait, calling out who he was, until the door was opened a chink and he was allowed in.

Eachann stood trembling before the chief and made a full confession. There was a wave of relief in the castle, ending in laughter; and Eachann was allowed a free pardon for his action in view of the entertainment he had provided. Puzzled by the whole affair, and quite unknowing about the thief hanging in the wood, he returned to his home and went to bed. However, when all this was going on, Seumas decided after his long wait that the game was really up with watchers moving all around, so he resolved to go through the wood and contact Eachann. But as he stumbled through in the darkness he ran right into the hanging corpse. Recoiling, and seeing the glint of the red beard, he cried out "Oh, poor Eachann. I'm too late. They've caught you and made an end of you when I was waiting. This is what we get for listening to our chattering wives. But stop you; the least I can do is to cut you down and take you back to your wife."

This he did, carrying the heavy body all the way to Eachann's house. Bean Eachann was inconsolable, with loud lamentations when she saw what she took to be her husband's body lying outside in the dark. "Be quiet," said Seumas, "Before I tell you the story we must bury Eachann in the potato patch before the chief's men get here and do the same to us." So they dug a deep hole in the potato patch, reverently lowered the body in and covered it up. Seumas then rushed away home to give his wife the tragic news. When Eachann, returning much relieved from the castle arrived home, he found the door bolted against him . However much he knocked and hammered, his cowering wife inside refused to move, until in a rage he roared "Open the door; it's me, Eachann!" This made matters worse. "Away you go to your place under the earth," the poor woman quavered.

Eachann gave up and decided to seek sanctuary at the house of Seumas, who, he assumed, had escaped and returned home. Seumas and his wife were asleep by that time. When Eachann knocked repeatedly at Seumas's door without an answer, he wondered if everyone had lost their senses. At last Seumas got up and asked nervously who was there. The answer made Eachann feel that indeed there was some kind of buidseachd (sorcery) on him. "Ye'll no get in; I had enough of you when I carried you home from the wood on my back." "Is it you or me that's daft?" shouted Eachann furiously. "Get you a candle and you will see that it's myself - Eachann."

A candle was lit, and sure enough Seumas saw the undoubted figure of his comrade outside, with no sign of earth or hanging on him. So he opened the door, his wife made up the fire and soon they had untangled the whole affair, although they still had no idea of the identity of the third man. They decided to go together next day and throw themselves on the mercy of the chief.

Next day, the chief nearly choked with laughter when they told him the whole story. As they had both made such a frank confession, he forgave them; in fact, he arranged for Seumas to have the annual gift of an ox as well . . . something he might have been given right at the start if they were not in such awe of their chief!

A FAMILY STORY

If you ever manage across to the island of Inch Kenneth that was once second in sanctity to Iona, you will see a handsomely carved effigy of Sir Alan MacLean over his grave. One of the feet has been broken off. This happened in the 1860s when my father and his brothers and sisters were youngsters running about the island, of which my grandfather was manager. My father was blamed for damaging the carving. Even as late as when he was a father himself, he was still smarting under the accusation which earned him a thrashing. He told me that he had had nothing to do with it. The damage had been caused by a cow either leaning against it, or rubbing itself on Sir Alan's foot!

THE PEDLAR'S POOL

I began with the sad story of the young couple who lost their lives in such a tragic fashion. I finish with another sad story of a man who gave his life for strangers. At Ardura, beside Loch Spelve, is the handsome memorial to Mull's greatest poet Dugald MacPhail (built in the 1920s with stones taken from his old house). The old road keeps left along the windings of the river Lussa up sunny Strath Coil almost as far as Torness, with the fine new road cutting along the hillside well above. A walk up the old road through the wood, peaceful, with only the rush of the river beside you, takes you after two miles or so to a small but deep pool under a rocky bluff where the old road rises and winds around it. Just beside the pool, almost hidden by the trees, there stands a substantial cairn surmounted by an iron Celtic cross bearing the words - 'John Jones died 1st April 1891'.

Jones was a pedlar, a travelling packman, people who were always welcomed for the gossip and news they brought to isolated communities. His rounds took him to Bunessan, where he was told with some fear that two households had been smitten with the smallpox. This was a disease regarded with almost superstitious horror, and even towards the end of the 19th century there were still isolated outbreaks. People refused to go near infected houses, but usually left food and necessities to be collected by the victims, if they were able The dead were handled in the fumes of burning tar, the bodies rolled into a tarpaulin with the least handling.

To this scene came John Jones, the pedlar. Without hesitation, he entered the infected houses, nursed and helped the victims until the disease had run its course. Then he resumed his rounds. But halting here, in the hollow beside the pool, he found he had been infected so seriously that he died all alone and was found and interred together with his pack, and above his grave the cairn was erected to his memory. Ever since that little salmon pool has been known as the Pedlar's Pool.